For over one hundred years, the Statue of Liberty has stood in New York Harbor, facing out to sea and holding high a burning torch. It is a colossal statue, the tallest statue in the world, 305 feet from the base of its pedestal to the tip of its torch. The statue is an amazing feat of sculpture and engineering. The massive, solid-looking figure is actually made of a thin layer of pounded copper—a kind of metal skin. Inside the hollow statue stands a vast iron-and-steel framework, a skeleton, to hold up the metal skin. The most impressive thing about this statue, however, is not the way it was built, but how powerfully it conveys the idea of freedom to people all over the world.

The Statue of Liberty symbolizes freedom to people all over the world.

Frédéric Auguste Bartholdi, the artist who created the Statue of Liberty

The artist who made the statue, Frédéric Auguste Bartholdi, named it *Liberty Enlightening the World.* He designed the statue in 1875 as a monument to American independence. At the statue's feet, he put a broken chain to show that the United States had broken free from Great Britain's rule. In her left arm, Liberty carries a tablet with the date of the Declaration of Independence, July 4, 1776, written on it in Roman numerals. This is because the Declaration of Independence launched the great American experiment; the founding of a republic where people govern themselves.

Bartholdi hoped that the success of this republic would be an example for the rest of the

Cornerstones of Freedom

The Statue of Liberty

Natalie Miller

CHILDREN'S PRESS
A Division of Grolier Publishing
Sherman Turnpike
Danbury, Connecticut 06816

Library of Congress Cataloging-in-Publication Data

Miller, Natalie.
  The Statue of Liberty / by Natalie Miller.

    p.   cm.—(Cornerstones of freedom)
  Summary: Describes Auguste Bartholdi's conception of
the Statue of Liberty, its construction in France, and its
eventual erection and dedication in New York Harbor.
  IBSN 0-516-06655-2
  1. Statue of Liberty (New York, N.Y.)—Juvenile
literature. 2. New York (N.Y.)—Buildings, structures,
etc.—Juvenile literature. [1. Statue of Liberty (New York,
N.Y.) 2. National monuments. 3. Statues. 4. Bartholdi,
Frédéric Auguste, 1834-1904.] I. Title, II. Series.
F128.64.L6M49 1992   91-44647
974.7'1—dc20   CIP
                                         AC

world. That is why Liberty holds a burning torch in her right hand and wears a crown with seven rays. Bartholdi hoped that the American belief in individual human worth and dignity would spread across the seven seas to the seven continents and light up the world.

Bartholdi himself was not an American; he was a Frenchman. The idea of creating a monument to America's independence first came up at a dinner party Bartholdi attended in 1865. The party was at the home of his friend, Édouard de Laboulaye. Laboulaye was a well-known teacher and writer. He had written several books about the United States. At his dinner party, conversation turned to the friendship between France and the United States. During the American Revolution, France had helped the struggling Americans win their independence from Great Britain. The two nations both cherished the same ideals. When the French people revolted against their country's oppressive monarchy in 1789, their battle cry had been, "Liberty, Equality, Fraternity!"

It was Laboulaye who suggested that a monument be built in the United States "by united effort [as] if it were a common work of both nations." The idea excited Bartholdi. He was already known in France for his monumental sculptures. A project like this one would offer a wonderful opportunity for him.

A famous date appears on the tablet held by Liberty.

Édouard de Laboulaye

5

In spite of his enthusiasm, Bartholdi was not able to start the project for several years. In 1865, the political situation in France was not favorable to such an undertaking. At the time, France was being ruled with an iron hand by Emperor Napoleon III. He might have been angered by the idea of building a statue that glorified the concept of human liberty. Bartholdi did not let this discourage him. He wrote of his planned statue, "I will try to glorify the Republic and Liberty over there, in the hope that someday I will find it again here." France was also edging toward war with Germany. Bartholdi fought in this war when it broke out in 1870. After the war, he again went to discuss the idea with Laboulaye. They agreed that Bartholdi should travel to America to see the country, meet some of its people, and gauge whether Americans would be interested in such a joint project.

Bartholdi bought passage on the *Pereire*, a big steamship that churned across the Atlantic in thirteen days. Many of the passengers on Bartholdi's ship were immigrants, people leaving their homes to start a new life in America. As the ship steamed into New York Harbor, the passengers crowded the deck to get a first sight of the city. Guarding the entrance to the harbor was tiny Bedloe's Island. As soon as he saw this island, Bartholdi knew it was the ideal spot for his statue. Standing here in the harbor, his statue

As soon as Bartholdi saw Bedloe's Island (shown here as it looks today), he knew it was the perfect spot for his statue.

could welcome travelers with a powerful image of the freedom they had come far to find.

Bartholdi spent five months traveling through the United States. He journeyed from New York to California and back, all the while talking with Americans and showing his drawings. If the French people made a gift of the statue, would the Americans provide the land and build a pedestal for it? The people he spoke with, including some influential congressmen and President Grant himself, liked the idea. When Bartholdi boarded his ship back to France, he was convinced that the plan would work.

Left: Charlotte Bartholdi, who inspired the final version of the statue's face
Right: A bronze of the first model for the statue's head
Below: One of the earliest clay models of the statue

It would be four more years before he would be able to begin. Bartholdi kept the idea alive until 1875, when the political situation in France had become stable enough for people to take an interest in his project. Bartholdi first made a four-foot-tall clay model that he showed to Laboulaye and his friends. They pledged to raise the money to pay for the statue if Bartholdi would build it. Both tasks would prove harder than they expected.

Bartholdi set to work making a series of clay models, changing the crown, the face, the torch, the pose of the figure. With the sixth clay statue, he finally had a design that he liked. (The final design for Liberty's face closely resembles the face of Bartholdi's mother.) The next task was to enlarge his design, step by step, keeping all the

An engraving of Bartholdi's studio showing a series of increasingly larger plaster models of the statue's right hand

parts of the huge final figure in proportion. First he made a 9-foot-tall plaster model; then he measured each part very carefully and expanded the measurements to make a plaster model 36 feet tall. Bartholdi and his assistants kept measuring and building larger and larger plaster figures until he had a model as big as the final statue. No building in Paris was large enough to hold a 151-foot-tall statue, so Bartholdi had to build the final plaster model in huge sections that would fit inside his warehouse studio.

Once the plaster sections were made, the workmen made big wooden forms that followed the shape of the plaster pieces exactly. Finally, they laid big, flat sheets of copper inside the wooden forms and hammered the copper into the smooth curves and lines of the statue's form. Bartholdi's warehouse was a busy and confusing place to a visitor. The air was full of plaster dust, sawdust, and the noise of hammering. Sections of the statue lay about like pieces of a monstrous puzzle. In all, it took one hundred tons of copper to make the statue's outer skin.

Meanwhile, raising enough money to buy materials and to pay all of Bartholdi's workmen was proving to be a difficult job as well. The fund-raisers had started to ask for donations in

Construction of the full-scale plaster model of Liberty's left arm

Metalworkers form sections of Liberty's copper "skin."

1875. They needed an amount equal to four hundred thousand American dollars. Donations came in from individuals, businesses, and towns, but three years later, the fund was far short of the needed amount. The committee finally hit on an idea that worked. They held a huge lottery offering five hundred prizes. Everyone who took a chance on the lottery would also be helping to pay for the statue. By 1881, the French had raised enough money to complete the statue. Now it was up to the Americans to do their part.

By this time, Bartholdi's grand project had been largely forgotten by Americans. In 1876, Bartholdi sent them a big reminder. The year 1876 marked the hundredth anniversary of the American Declaration of Independence. Although

Bartholdi was not able to finish the entire statue in time for the celebration, he did manage to complete the right hand. In August 1876, the hand was sent to America and put on display at the International Exhibition in Philadelphia. Nine hundred thousand people stopped to wonder at it. The hand and torch were thirty feet tall. One finger was taller than a man; a single fingernail was more than a foot across. If the hand was this big, the people realized with awe, the finished statue would be colossal indeed. People paid fifty cents to climb stairs up to the balcony surrounding the torch. The price of admission, of course, went to help pay for the statue.

After the hand was finished and shipped to America, Bartholdi began working on the statue's head. Each day, many curious onlookers came to watch the workmen, looking like dwarfs, running up the scaffolding to pound on a lip a yard wide or shape a single curl that was higher than a room. Liberty's head was finished in time to go to the Paris World Fair in 1878. Bartholdi walked nervously beside the sturdy wagon, pulled by twelve strong horses, that carried the precious cargo to the fairgrounds.

Bartholdi was an expert sculptor; he knew how to make the huge statue. But he did not know how to support it; how to keep it from swaying and cracking in the strong winds of New York

The statue's head was exhibited at the 1878 Paris World Fair.

Alexandre Gustave Eiffel

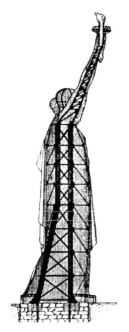

Eiffel's support system for the statue

Harbor. For this, he needed the help of a famous French engineer, Alexandre Gustave Eiffel. At the time, Eiffel was known in France as a designer of bridges. Later, he would become world famous for building the Eiffel Tower in Paris.

Eiffel designed a special skeleton to support Bartholdi's statue. The main support was a central tower made of four thick, vertical, iron beams. Horizontal and diagonal iron bars held the beams together. Extending out from the tower in every direction were hundreds of iron bars. The bars were attached to a network of steel "ribs" that curved and bent to follow the shape of the statue's inner surface. The ribs were then riveted to the inside of Liberty's copper "skin." This way, the thin outer skin would not be carrying its own weight. Instead, it would be suspended, like a curtain, from the skeleton. This design worked wonderfully because it was strong, but at the same time, it had some give. It was flexible enough to allow the statue to twist and sway a little bit in a strong wind. Also, when the summer sun beat down on the statue, some pieces would heat up and expand more than others. Eiffel's structure allowed the different parts of the statue to expand and contract separately without cracking the statue or splitting its joints.

Eiffel and his workmen built the steel skeleton on a platform just outside Bartholdi's warehouse.

In 1883, workers began putting the statue together in a courtyard outside Bartholdi's Paris workshop.

In 1883, they began to put the statue together. Starting with Liberty's feet, the workmen began riveting the large pieces of copper skin to the iron-and-steel skeleton. The scaffolding went higher and higher as they worked their way up the statue. One day, twenty newsmen were invited to the studio. Bartholdi quickly led them through piles of wire and copper to a door in the lady's sandal. Up, up, up they climbed. Huffing and puffing, the newsmen were glad to stop on a platform, where they found a table set with

The old, star-shaped fort that stood on Bedloe's Island was used as a foundation for the statue's pedestal.

dishes. "Gentlemen," said Bartholdi, "I welcome you to lunch in the knee of my big daughter, Liberty."

By the end of the year, the statue was finished. All the pieces fit together beautifully. She stood looking down on the roofs of Paris, waiting patiently to go to her new home. But her home was not ready for her.

It had been twelve years since Bartholdi first proposed his plan in the United States. In that time, the U.S. Congress had voted to set aside Bedloe's Island for the statue. An American architect, Richard Morris Hunt, had designed a pedestal for the statue. He planned to repair the walls of an old, star-shaped fort that stood on the island and use it as a foundation for the pedestal. But in 1883, as Liberty stood completed in Paris, work on the pedestal had not even begun. Construction finally did begin in 1884, but before the base was even half finished, all work suddenly came to a halt. There was no money to complete the project. People across the United States did not understand that Liberty was a gift to all the American people. They thought of it as a lighthouse for New York City and did not want to pay for the pedestal. It was New York's gift, they said.

Richard Morris Hunt

Work on the statue's pedestal began in 1884.

Joseph Pulitzer

Meanwhile, in Paris, Bartholdi and his men began to take the statue apart and pack it, section by section, in 214 huge crates. Finally, New York newspaper owner Joseph Pulitzer decided to use his paper, *The World*, to help Liberty's cause. He wrote articles asking for donations, no matter how small. He promised to print the name of every single person who gave money to the pedestal fund. He persuaded newspaper editors in other towns to join the campaign. Thousands of small donations began to pour in—many of them less than a dollar. But in five months, all these small amounts added up to $100,000. By August 1885, there was enough money to finish the pedestal.

Appealing for donations to the pedestal fund, this 1885 cartoon bore the caption: "Even Liberty demands something substantial to stand upon."

On July 11, 1885, cheering spectators crowded onto Bedloe's Island to greet the French ship Isére, *which had carried the disassembled statue across the Atlantic in 214 huge crates.*

The statue itself had already arrived, two months before. The 214 crates carrying Bartholdi's statue and Eiffel's framework sat in storage on Bedloe's Island waiting while workmen finished framing and pouring twenty-seven tons of concrete to form the statue's base. The crates sat unopened for nearly a year; the pedestal wasn't ready until April 1886. To honor all the citizens who had sent small donations, the workers mixed pennies, nickels, and dimes into the wet mortar used to lay the last stone in the pedestal.

By the end of September 1886, only the head and torch were not yet in place.

Next came the difficult task of putting the statue together. The people on the shore watched curiously as each day, the strange skeleton rose higher into the sky. Then, the copper skin was attached to the skeleton with three hundred thousand copper rivets. Workers hurried to assemble Liberty's head and torch in time for the unveiling ceremony.

The completed statue looked splendid. Liberty's face was veiled with a huge French flag that was to be removed during the ceremony. The scaffolding was dismantled in time for the dedication day, October 28, 1886.

It was a cold, rainy day. But that did not keep away the thousands who lined the streets of New York to watch the long parade. Bartholdi, standing next to President Cleveland, enjoyed every bit of it. He did not even mind when they found there would not be time for lunch before going to the island for the dedication ceremony. Ships waiting at the southern tip of Manhattan carried Bartholdi and other invited guests out to Bedloe's Island. Hundreds of thousands of spectators watched from the shore in New York and New Jersey. Thousands more watched from boats of all sizes crowding into the harbor.

The celebration of the statue's unveiling

Visitors view the harbor from the statue's torch in the late 1800s.

At two o'clock, Bartholdi climbed the steps to the top of his statue. He waited impatiently for the signal to pull the cord that would drop the French flag from its face. When he heard a round of applause far below, during New York senator William Evarts's speech, he thought it was his signal. Bartholdi pulled the cord. When the hundreds of gaily decorated ships in the harbor saw the veil fall, they tooted their whistles all at once. Bands played, people cheered, and cannons boomed a twenty-one-gun salute. No one heard the end of Mr. Evarts's speech.

Americans were delighted with this French gift. In 1883, a young woman named Emma Lazarus had written a poem, "The New Colossus," about the Statue of Liberty. In her poem, Lazarus calls the statue the "Mother of Exiles" and imagines her saying these words:

Emma Lazarus

> Give me your tired, your poor,
> Your huddled masses yearning to breathe free,
> The wretched refuse of your teeming shore.
> Send these, the homeless, tempest-tost to me.
> I lift my lamp beside the golden door!

For millions of immigrants who arrived in New York Harbor, the Statue of Liberty became a symbol of hope.

During World War I, Liberty's image appeared on posters urging support for the war effort.

Millions of immigrants came to the United States in the late nineteenth and early twentieth centuries, and the poem seemed to capture the newcomers' feelings about the statue. In 1903, a bronze plaque inscribed with the poem was added to the base of the statue. In the 1960s, a museum dedicated to the history of American immigration was opened inside the pedestal.

During World War I, the United States War Department was in charge of the statue. The war department decided to make the torch shine brighter as a gesture of hope for the millions fighting in Europe. In 1916, hundreds of windows were cut in the torch's flame and powerful lights were installed inside. The torch

By the 1970s, many parts of the statue, including the torch, were in desperate need of repair.

did glow more brightly, but the new windows also leaked. Gradually, the iron ribs inside the torch and the right arm rusted. By the 1970s, the supports inside the torch were so weakened and damaged by rust that the torch seemed ready to break off. When assembling the statue in 1886, workers had mistakenly attached the head and the right arm about two feet out of line with the original design. As a result, the supports for Liberty's right arm were never as strong as Eiffel had intended them to be. By the late 1970s,

By the 1940s, the inside of Liberty's crown was covered with graffiti.

Liberty's shoulder was in need of a major repair. Moreover, Liberty's head had tilted until one point of her crown was threatening to poke a hole through the copper skin of the right arm.

Over the years, the salty, polluted air of New York Harbor had also eaten away at the statue. Liberty's copper skin was stained by corrosion on the outside and covered with patches of graffiti on the inside. In 1924, the statue had been declared a national monument. The National Park Service was placed in charge of it in 1933. Since that time, some repairs had been made, but by the 1970s, preserving the statue had become a massive problem.

Just as two Frenchmen, Bartholdi and Laboulaye, had taken the lead in creating the monument, it was two Frenchmen who led the drive to preserve the Statue of Liberty. In 1980, an engineer named Jacques Moutard was repairing an old statue in France. This statue, though much smaller than Liberty, was also made of a copper skin over an iron skeleton. Seeing the damage to the French statue made Moutard wonder about the condition of the Statue of Liberty. He discussed this with Philippe Vallery-Radot, a wealthy friend and supporter. Together, they contacted the United States National Park Service and drew up a plan to repair the great statue in time for her hundredth anniversary in 1986.

In 1981, Moutard and American architect Richard Hayden led a team of French and American engineers who examined the statue, inside and out, and made a list of all the needed repairs. At the outset, they discovered that all the original plans and drawings had been lost. They had to begin by making detailed drawings of every part of the statue, just to keep track of where the repairs were needed. Carrying out this time-consuming and detailed job cost $5 million. The repairs themselves would probably cost another $30 million.

Once the scope of the project was known, President Ronald Reagan formed a commission to raise money. The commission launched an advertising campaign, and the American people began to send in donations. As the fund grew, the

*The old torch (above) was removed and replaced with a replica
that faithfully follows Bartholdi's original design.*

*Liberty during
restoration*

repairs began. In 1984, workmen carefully surrounded the statue with a 305-foot-tall scaffold. The designers took precautions with the scaffold. Even in a 100-mile-an-hour wind, it would sway only three inches; to be safe, there was an eighteen-inch gap between the statue and the scaffold at every point.

Inside the statue, workers cleaned off paint and rust with liquid nitrogen. The iron ribs that lined the statue's skin were removed and replaced with stainless-steel ribs. This job required careful planning. Each of the eighteen hundred ribs had a different shape. The steel replacements had to match the original iron ribs exactly. Moreover, to avoid leaving the statue unsupported, only four ribs could be replaced at a time.

Outside, the head was gently tipped back into place, away from the right arm. Helicopters lifted away the corroded torch and, in November 1985, a new one was raised in its place. Like the original torch, the new one is made of thin, pounded copper sheets. Its flame, however, has no windows and is covered with gold leaf. Instead of being lighted from within, it is lighted from the outside by sixteen powerful floodlights located around the torch's rim. By the beginning of 1986, the repairs were complete. All that remained was to dismantle the elaborate scaffolding.

On July 3, 1986, everything was ready for Liberty's centennial celebration. That evening,

President Reagan was on hand at Liberty's centennial celebration.

French president François Mitterand joined President Ronald Reagan for the relighting ceremony. Americans all over the country watched live television coverage of the event as a laser beam relit the torch. On the Fourth of July, there was a parade of twenty-two tall ships in the bay and an extravagant fireworks show. America truly honored Liberty's hundredth birthday.

On July 5, the statue, which had been closed during repairs, was reopened to visitors. Before the repairs, climbing the fifteen stories up to the observation windows in Liberty's crown had been a strenuous experience. After riding an elevator to the top of the pedestal, visitors advanced, step by step, up a spiral staircase that wound up through the statue. As one looked up, the entire staircase bristled with people on each of the 171 steps. Once a person began the climb, there were very few chances to step out of line to rest or catch a breath of air. On hot days, the sun heated up the copper statue, and the temperature inside could rise to over 100 degrees.

Part of the aim of the restoration had been to make this climb safer and more pleasant for visitors. A new emergency elevator now ran from the base of the statue all the way up to its shoulder. The stairs had been repaired; the banister replaced. The rest areas along the way were improved, and an air-conditioning system was installed.

A dazzling fireworks display was the finale to Liberty's birthday celebration.

Since its arrival in 1886, Bartholdi's *Liberty Enlightening the World* has been a beloved national symbol. For millions of immigrants, Liberty was an instantly recognizable image of the freedom and the opportunity they hoped to find in America. The restoration of the Statue of Liberty was one way of showing that America's pride in and love of that ideal is still alive and strong.

INDEX

PHOTO CREDITS

Cover, © Bill Frakes/SharpShooters; 1, 2, 3, © SuperStock; 4, AP/Wide World; 5 (top), Photri; 5 (bottom),
Historical Pictures/Stock Montage; 7, Photri; 8 (top left), National Park Service: Statue of Liberty National
Monument; 8 (top right, bottom), 9, Museum of the City of New York; 10, 11, Rare Books and
Manuscripts Division, The New York Public Library, Astor, Lenox and Tilden Foundations; 12, Museum
of the City of New York; 13, AP/Wide World; 14 (both photos), Historical Pictures/Stock Montage; 15
(both photos), Rare Books and Manuscripts Division, The New York Public Library, Astor, Lenox and
Tilden Foundations; 16, SuperStock; 17 (top), North Wind; 17 (bottom), Historical Pictures/Stock
Montage; 18 (top), AP/Wide World; 18 (bottom), North Wind; 19, Museum of the City of New York; 20, 21,
Historical Pictures/Stock Montage; 22, North Wind; 23 (top), AP/Wide World; 23 (bottom), SuperStock;
24, AP/Wide World; 25, Photri; 26, AP/Wide World; 28 (top), Statue of Liberty-Ellis Island Foundation; 28
(bottom), © SuperStock; 29 (both photos), © Jeff Perkell/Amstock; 31, © SuperStock

Picture Identifications:
Cover: The Statue of Liberty
Page 1: The Statue of Liberty and the New York skyline at night
Page 2: Liberty and the New York skyline at dusk

Project Editor: Shari Joffe
Designer: Karen Yops
Cornerstones of Freedom Logo: David Cunningham

ABOUT THE AUTHOR

Natalie Miller was born in Maine, grew up in Massachusetts, and majored in history at Beaver College
in Pennsylvania. She has written several titles in the *Cornerstones of Freedom* series for Childrens Press.